ALL ACTION
MOUNTAIN
BIKING

Withdrawn

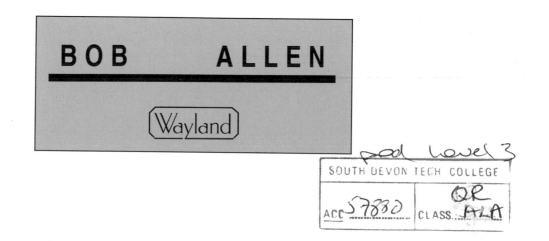

BOB ALLEN

Wayland

Titles in this series
Back packing
Canoeing
Climbing
Mountain biking
Skiing
Street skating
Survival skills
Wind and surf

All photographs are reproduced by kind permission of Bob Allen apart from *back cover* (Michele Dieterich), 4 and 11 (both Geoff Parr), 22 (Mountin' Excitement), 31 and 43 *right* (Eye Ubiquitous).

Front cover: A lone wild thing on the run in California.

Series editor: Paul Mason
Designer: Bridgewater Design/ Kudos Design

First published in 1991 by
Wayland (Publishers) Ltd
61 Western Rd, Hove
East Sussex BN3 1JD, England

© Copyright 1991 Wayland (Publishers) Limited

British Library Cataloguing in Publication Data
Allen, Bob
   Mountain biking
   1. Mountainous regions. Cycling
   I. Title II. Series
   796.609143

HARDBACK   ISBN 0-7502-0182-7

PAPERBACK   ISBN 0-7502-0467-2

Typeset by Malcolm Walker of Kudos Design
Printed by Rotolito Lombarda.
Bound by A.G.M., France.

Contents

BEGINNINGS

I t is hard to imagine life before mountain bikes. From crowded city streets to isolated mountain peaks, they are everywhere. You cannot open a magazine or walk into a bike shop without the colour and excitement of the sport grabbing your attention. It has captured the imagination of a whole new generation of riders. From the very young to the very old, this sport can offer fun in the sun (or the mud, or the snow) to anyone who gives it a go.

Not so long ago there was no such thing as a mountain bike. Although the idea of riding off the road has been around since the first bicycle, it took some overgrown kids from northern California to spark the

LEFT

Proof that the mountain bike really can go anywhere!

revolution that has created today's mountain bike. What started as a downhill race among friends in Marin County, California has become one of the world's fastest growing and most popular sports.

The riders who gathered for the first downhill dash wore jeans and heavy shirts and rode bicycles made of whatever parts they could find lying on the garage floor. They met at the top of a trail they called Repack. It was called this because the trail was so steep that the riders who used coaster brakes had to repack them after they overheated. Heavy old Schwinn frames were a favourite among these downhill pioneers. There were no rules about what the bikes should look like. But you might not recognize one as an ancestor of one of today's mountain bikes!

The first mountain bikers quickly found out that the heavy duty parts and frames they needed did not exist. They went on to build some of the first mountain bikes. Many of them are still building bikes and continually bringing new ideas and products to mountain biking.

The outcome is a style of bike and riding that has captured the imagination of a whole generation of adventurers. The speed and excitement of cycling on the road are combined with the freedom to go where you want, across some of the roughest country in the world. You could be grinding up a slope, taking it to the limit on a descent or doing a slalom through a forest. Whichever you choose, you will find that the

Gary Fisher was one of the downhill pioneers who raced the Repack in Marin County, California. His old Schwinn was one of the first clunkers put together from bits and pieces. Some of Fisher's ideas helped to form today's mountain bikes, and through his design and manufacturing company he is still at the forefront of the mountain biking world.

LEFT

The perfect
getaway vehicle for
a mail deliverer -
the dog just can't
keep up.

spirit of adventure that started mountain biking is still at the heart of the sport.

Total confidence in your ability and the realization that you are only limited by your imagination are things that are necessary to any sport. To ride a mountain bike down a radical descent, ski through a mogul field or surf in monster waves you have to believe you can do it. If you are not sure, you will probably fail.

So why bother with mountain biking? There are probably as many reasons as there are riders. The UK Womens' Champion, Deb Murrell, got into mountain biking because of a dream.

'All I wanted was a horse when I was young but I couldn't have one.

I started riding a woman's shopper bike in the hills pretending it was a horse. I would tear up and down the bridle ways doing things which that bike wasn't capable of surviving. I didn't think about it, I just did it. I'd get covered in mud and love it. The great thing was just being outside.'

RIGHT

Deb Murrell, one of the UK's best riders, started riding a bike because she couldn't have a horse.

BELOW

The balance you use skating is useful for mountain biking.

World Champion John Tomac gained much of his superior handling skill from riding BMX. *'I started out in BMX at four years old and was racing by seven. I practised every day.'* Every time Tomac races he is using the skills he developed when he was riding no further than his back yard at a very young age.

From the moment you took your first steps, you were starting to learn how to ride a bike. Climbing trees,

LEFT

The thrill of a fast ride through a forest.

running and jumping all develop the balance and co-ordination used in mountain biking. Even if you have never ridden a bike before, other experiences help develop your natural ability and become a base for your mountain biking skills. Any cycling you have done will be useful when you start riding off road.

It is not the bike but the attitude you have when you ride it that counts.

You could be riding a BMX or an old shopping bike; the only trouble is that it might fall apart in places that a specialized mountain bike would not. Mountain biking is about going out with a bunch of friends, racing around neighbourhood trails, getting dirty and having fun. Mountain bikes have broken the restraints of the road and made the biking world an endless adventure. So get out there and ride!

MACHINERY

ABOVE

Not so hi-tech. This bike had nails through its tyres for grip.

LEFT

A suspension system for mountain bikes.

can get muddled. Buy a bike made by a company that specializes in mountain bikes, then you will be sure you are getting a bike that will do the job properly.

Having a flash bike might impress your friends, but your riding skills are what really count. You do not have more fun because you spent more money. Sometimes you can get cheap second-hand bikes, but do not buy one without having someone who knows about bikes with you to check that it is a good buy. Check out the newspaper's classified ads or the board at the local bike shop to see what is available. An experienced mechanic should look at the bike before you part with any money. Some bikes need only minor adjustments. Others have hidden damage.

Once you decide that you are going to buy a mountain bike, do not just buy the first one you try. Find out which one is best for you and your purse. Look at as many bikes as you can, to see what is available. Most of all, do not be confused by advertising hype. There are so many sizes, shapes and components to choose from, even experienced riders

The most important thing to think about when looking for a bike is that it is the right size. When standing over the top tube of the bike, you should have at least 5 cm clearance between the tube and your crotch. Do not let someone try to sell you a bike that is too big by claiming you will grow into it. Riding a bike that is too

RIGHT

A young rider on a bike with a dropped top tube, designed for smaller people.

big is very dangerous. When you are in traffic or on the trail, you need to be able to balance by putting a foot on the ground without tipping the bike.

Many cycle companies build mountain bikes for small people. The problem of stand-over height is solved either by fitting small wheels or designing a top tube which slopes down, or both. A bike with a sloping top tube and full size twenty-six-inch (65 cm) wheels is more easily modified to fit you as you grow.

It seems as though almost everyone is wearing flashy tight-fitting cycling clothes. These are a good way for manufacturers to make money, but you do not really need them to go mountain biking. Baggy shorts and T-shirts, or sweat-pants and sweat-shirts, are fine for riding.

If you start to ride often, there are some clothes you might want to invest in to make riding a bit more comfortable. Cycling shorts with seamless padding in the crotch will stop your backside from hurting on a long ride. A pair of padded cycling gloves stop your hands getting too sore. Whatever you buy, make sure you buy it because you need it, not because everyone else has got one. Mountain biking is about how you ride, not what you wear.

The weight of a bike is important, but do not be too worried about how much components weigh. Most peoples' cycling would improve if they cut down on sweets to lose some body weight!

BELOW

The only specialist clothing most of these riders have on is a helmet.

TECHNIQUE

G ood riding style comes from riding. Experience builds on experience and soon you will be performing moves that you never thought possible. All it takes is practice and a desire to improve.

Start by getting a feel for how the bike stops. When riding a bike for the first time, check to see how the brakes are set up. Riders in the USA and Europe mount their rear brakes on the right side of the handlebar, while UK riders mount them on the left. One method is not better than the other, but make sure you know how the bike is set up. There is no quicker way to fly over your handlebars than to pull on the front brake instead of the rear.

The brake levers should be set up so that when they are fully on they stop 2-3 cm from the bars. On long descents your hands get sore from a poor braking position. The braking grip needs to be as comfortable as possible from the start. Many riders hold the bars with two fingers and the levers with two. Then they can brake

14

quickly without losing grip over rough ground. Experiment to find out what hand position works best for you.

Before taking the bike off road, practice quick, sharp stops. Really squeeze on the brakes and feel how your weight is thrown forward. Anticipate the braking action by moving your weight back and bracing yourself with your arms. Use the front

Bicycles are one of the few things in life where you pay more for less. The top-line mountain bikes of today are very light. To build these featherweight machines, the builder uses hi-tech materials such as titanium, aluminium and carbon fibre to shave off the kilograms. Lightweight components and materials are expensive and add to the cost of a bike.

FAR LEFT and ABOVE

While descending, put your weight at the back of the bike. Be careful not to sit on the wheel!

and rear brakes together for the best stopping speed. The front brake is more powerful and must be used with care. When descending, the brakes should be lightly squeezed on and off so that they do not lock the wheels. This is called feathering. Remember that you need a lot more space to stop in if the rims are wet.

Accurate shifting and good pedalling technique are critical skills for offroad riding. The time lost by a missed shift can lose a race for even

RIGHT

The gears and rear derailleur. Try to remember which gear you are in without looking down.

the most experienced pros. And it could mean that you have to get off and push the bike up the hill.

Keep up a constant pedalling speed over different ground. Over long distances your body is more efficient if you pedal at higher speeds. Try a cadence of between sixty and eighty revolutions a minute. That is one spin a second or more. You might feel a bit stupid pedalling this fast, but you will develop a smooth cadence that makes cycling easier. Use the gears to keep pedalling at the same speed over different ground. To ride faster select the next higher gear and try to maintain your spin. Pushing too hard a gear wears you

out quicker and can damage your knees. Speed and strength come from a good steady spin.

The shifters mounted on the handlebars control the derailleurs that change gear. The front derailleur is controlled through the left shifter and moves the chain between different-sized chainrings on the crankset. The rear derailleur (the right shifter) moves the chain across the gears on the freewheel.

Avoid the extremes of gearing. The combination of either the big chainring to the large freewheel gear or the smallest chainring to the small gear in the back causes chain and tooth damage, which is very expensive to put right. Try to

RIGHT

In-the-saddle
climbing is best
for long climbs.

remember what gear you are in without looking down. If you do not watch the trail instead of the drive train you will end up sitting in the dirt!

Most shifting systems are not designed to be used under hard pedal pressure. So when you are climbing, you need to let off the pressure just long enough to shift gears. This does not mean stop pedalling! Just ease off a bit. If noises come from the gears after shifting, move the levers a bit until they stop. You soon learn how to recognize noises and adjust the gears so that the individual sounds quickly disappear.

CLIMBING

Climbing is an integral part of the sport because riding in the hills is what mountain biking is about. You can choose two techniques for climbing; riding in or out of the saddle. How good you are at climbing depends on how you shift your weight to control the way the tyres grip the ground. Out-of-the-saddle pedalling is for power on short, sharp climbs. On a long climb stay in the seat or you will quickly get tired.

Move your weight forward, by bending your arms to bring your upper body over the front of the bike and sitting further forward in the saddle. The combination of arm bending and saddle sliding will improve your climbing. Moving too far forward will reduce the rear wheel's grip and let it spin. Practice will teach you how you and your bike climb best.

'Gear down going into the climb and keep spinning as it gets steeper', advises UK Champion Tim Davies. *'Look ahead and anticipate what gears you'll need.'*

When the going gets tough you may find yourself walking with the bike. Pushing it is fine if the trail is smooth, but if it is rough and rocky you might have to carry it. It is best to carry the bike over your right shoulder so the oily chain stays away from

LEFT

Out-of-the-saddle climbing is best for short, fast bursts.

RIGHT

You might even have to carry the bike if the hill is steep.

'When I first started climbing, the front wheel would bounce off the ground and I'd fall off the back of the bike. I learned that by moving my weight forward I could maintain the right balance on the bike and control this unwanted (and painful!) wheelie.' Sally Hibberd, top racer.

your clothes. Reach through the main triangle with your right arm and lift the bike so the top tube rests on your shoulder. Steady the handlebars with your left hand. Fixing a pad around the top tube makes carrying much more comfortable.

DOWNHILLING

A fter a long, hard climb you have certainly earned the downhill to follow! Downhills are probably the most exciting aspect of mountain biking. They can also be the most dangerous. It is easy to accelerate out of control. So, do not speed down an unfamiliar trail. You never know what could be lurking there to throw you off the bike.

As the trail gets steeper you will need to move your weight backwards to keep in balance. Very steep sections can be negotiated by lowering your seat and really hanging over the back. Care must be taken not to drag your backside on the tyre. On such technical descents, speed is secondary to good technique. As your skills increase, the speed will naturally follow.

At the age of twenty-one a diving accident left David Constantine a quadriplegic. Since that time his life hasn't slowed down much. For his final project at the Royal College of Art in London, he designed and built a device which connects any mountain bike to a wheel chair. He is shown here using his invention.

Dave Wonderly,
professional rider,
controlling a slide.

shocks. Always ride in control and anticipate your next move. Ride with the crank arms parallel to the ground to keep the pedals above the rocks and ruts. It is important to have a good grip on the bars so that unexpected bumps don't tear your hands off.'

The high speed turns of a descent demand good technique. Wonderly attributes his downhill ability to, 'knowing how much speed you can take into a corner and still retain traction'. He feels it is good to, 'practise skidding into turns and learning to control the bike when a wheel slides. Feathering the brakes to prevent wheel lock up reduces the risk of sliding a wheel in a turn.'

As your skills progress, you may find the need for even trickier manoeuvres. Wheelies, front and rear wheel hops and balance can be perfected through practice. World Trials Champion, Hans Rey, suggests, 'get your friends together and make a game out of riding everything you see. Just by attempting difficult moves you'll automatically improve. Set up a neighbourhood championship to see who is best in your group.'

Dave Wonderly, one of the best downhill riders in the world, advises, 'Let your arms and legs support your body above the bike as it floats around underneath you absorbing the

PREPARATION

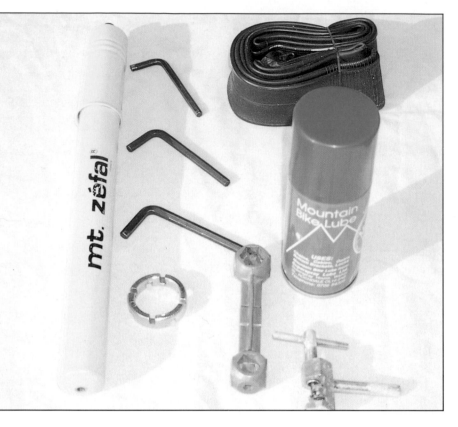

B efore every ride give the bike a quick check to make sure everything is working. If you have quick release hubs, check that the skewers are tight. Point the quick release levers to the back of the bike. This will stop a branch or rock accidentally opening it. Quick release hubs make it easier to take off wheels, and you will not need to carry a spanner to loosen wheel nuts. Make sure your tyres are pumped up and the brakes are working properly.

Take a basic tool kit on rides to make sure that you are not left shivering in the rain by a flat tyre or mechanical problem. You will need a spare inner tube, tyre levers to remove the tyre from the rim and a spanner. The most useful spanner is a multi-purpose tool that looks like a jack knife and contains allen keys and screwdrivers. Many riders carry this kit in a small pack under their seats. A pump should be fitted to the frame in a place where it will not interfere with riding or carrying the bike.

As well as the tools, your kit should include some money for emergencies. Take enough to buy

LEFT

Some of the tools you may need (clockwise): a pump, allen keys, a spare inner tube, lubricant, a chain splitter, a multi - headed spanner and a spoke key.

some food if you run out of energy and enough loose change for a phone call. Do not buy sweets with it! Somewhere in your gear you should have some sort of identification that gives your name, where you live, who to contact in case of an emergency and any medical conditions or allergies you might have. Accidents and injuries do happen sometimes, so be prepared. Most importantly, let someone know where you have gone for a ride and when you expect to be back.

Keep an eye on the weather and be prepared for quick changes. It is better to take too much clothing than too little. Extra clothes and food can

be carried in a bum bag. This sort of pack does not trap heat against your back, so it is more comfortable than a rucksack.

F it your bike with a water bottle cage to carry a drink, and take a full bottle on every ride. It is very important to drink a lot even when it is cold outside. Your body loses a lot of water when you are riding. Top it up! Otherwise your body runs low and you will quickly slow down or stop. When the weather is hot, drink liquid before, during and after a ride to make sure that you do not get dehydrated.

Deb Murrell warns, *'Young and*

LEFT

Make sure that the quick release is pointing backwards, so that it isn't pulled open when you are riding along.

ABOVE

Practise taking your water bottle out of the cage without looking.

without looking down. It is silly to lose control by looking at your water bottle.

If you do not know where to ride in your area, the local bike shop should know of places, or even better, of groups who go on regular rides. If there are no groups near you, get your friends together and start one. Riding with a bunch of friends brings out the competitive spirit. Do not worry if you fall behind older, more experienced riders. Think of it as a challenge. Every time you ride you will be a little stronger and soon you will be right up with them.

When riding with a group you must stop and let the slower members catch up. A flat tyre or mechanical problem could leave the missing person needing help. Each rider has a responsibility to the rest of the group. Everyone who started the ride must be there at the end. Remember, it could be you out there alone, so look out for each other.

Cycling fitness comes from riding and having fun on the bike. Each pedal stroke will make you fitter, stronger, and more skilful. Cycling endurance comes from regular training rides over greater distances.

novice riders don't drink enough water. They just don't realize how serious dehydration can be.' She suggests that, *'developing a habit of sipping water throughout a ride is very important. Try to finish every ride with an empty bottle.'*

Practise drinking while riding until you can remove and replace the bottle

ABOVE and
RIGHT

When out with a
group, watch out
for the other
riders. If you are
alone, don't take
any risks.

The longer and more often you ride, the fitter you become.

See if you are getting faster by timing your favourite ride. Every couple of weeks ride it as hard as you can. Your time will show how much you have improved.

A helmet should be worn whenever you are on the bike. Sally Hibberd admits that wearing a helmet, *'gives me the confidence to try things I would never dream of without it.'* While there are no excuses for not wearing one, you will still hear people saying that helmets are hot and uncomfortable or just not cool. When the statistics show that wearing one could save your life, it only makes sense. Hibberd adds, *'It becomes so natural to wear it, I forget it's on.'*

For those who enjoy competition, racing is the best part of mountain biking. Some people race to win, others just enjoy the competitive atmosphere and the friends they meet. Finishing a difficult race is very satisfying. It becomes a race against your own abilities.

Mountain bike races are usually held over two days with events and categories for all ages and ability levels. If you are not interested in a strenuous cross-country race, why not test your skills on a trials course or the downhill?

While the actual racing may not be

LEFT

A stock trials bike competition.

RIGHT

The cross-country race is usually the main event of a competition.

for everyone, you can learn a lot from going to a race and just watching. Mountain bike courses are great for spectators. Pick a difficult section of the cross-country course and watch how different riders handle the same technical problem. Do they climb in or out of the saddle? What gear are they in and when do they shift? Analyse the line they take through a high speed turn or a rocky descent. You will learn a lot.

The cross-country race is usually the main event for the weekend. This is the most demanding type of mountain bike competition. The courses combine gruelling uphills, rocky descents and stream crossings. They test the riders' endurance and technical skills to the limit. The races sometimes include up to 300 competitors. Having a fast start is important to avoid being trapped behind slower riders.

Some courses are just one long circuit, but most are six to ten kilometres long. Riders do a different number of laps depending what category they are racing in. Pro races are usually forty kilometres or longer and can take four hours. The riders must be prepared for mechanical failures because they cannot accept help or parts from anyone. If they get a flat or break a chain they have to fix it themselves with the tools they carry.

They can take food and drink from their team.

UK Champion Tim Davies admits that he is addicted to mountain biking. *'It's in my system and has become a way of life. I love racing.'* But he cautions young riders, *'Don't sacrifice everything for cycling too soon, especially not your education. A good education should be your first goal. Becoming a good racer is a long process so be patient.*

LEFT

UK champion Tim Davies, one of the growing number of professional riders.

RIGHT

Hans Rey, World Trials Champion three times, at a competition in California, USA.

'Don't expect to be winning right away. Let your body develop and don't overdo it. Ride to enjoy it.'

A trials competition is the ultimate test of the bike handling skills and concentration of a rider.

Boulders, fallen trees and other natural obstacles are part of a trials course. The competition consists of a number of short technical sections which the riders must negotiate. Points are taken off the rider's score each time her or his foot touches the ground, or 'dabs', with a maximum of five points taken off for falling out of bounds. The rider who has the least 'dabs' after everyone has ridden all the sections wins.

There are two kinds of trials bike. Stock trials bikes have a frame which has twenty-six-inch (65 centimetre) wheels and a functional rear derailleur

LEFT

The only sure way to get through the traffic. Boing! Boing! Boing!

to qualify. All other bikes fall into the open category, where anything goes. Trials bikes have heavy-duty forks and wheels to withstand the pounding they must endure. The show-offs of the sport always gather a crowd to witness their gravity-defying hops, twists and turns over steep cliffs and large boulders.

Hans Rey, who has three times been World Champion trials rider, stresses, *'You have to have the basics mastered on the ground before you can perform them three metres up on a boulder. Don't get frustrated by what you see others doing. Start easy then work up. You can't rush the learning process. It just takes practice, lots of it.'*

Often races will include either an uphill or downhill time trial or both. These races are usually against the clock. Riders are started individually and ride for the fastest time.

Uphill time trials are usually four to six kilometres long. The courses can climb a thousand metres. Just because they are short does not mean they are easy. It is a relatively quick race, so there is no holding back. Riders give their all from bottom to top. It takes concentration and

determination to block out the pain and just keep hammering up.

On the flip side, a downhill race can be the most action-packed event with plenty of thrills and spills. Riding at speed requires total concentration and complete belief in your bike and abilities. One small mistake can lead to incredible crashes and sometimes serious injuries. Usually the best riders wear shoulder, elbow and knee pads. Most are glad they do.

What started as a game between bored competitors waiting for a race award ceremony at the 1989 UK Championships grew into an organized contest at every race meeting. The first attempts were over a bent stick that soon evolved into a hopometer. The world record is a hyperhop of over a metre.

A LIZARD SINGS

A lmost anywhere there are hills to ride there will be downhill races. A fast descent is a test of sanity and handling abilities. Some of the most famous downhill races are in Northern California where the mountain bike was born. The Repack in Marin County and the Kamikazee at the Mammoth Mountain ski resort are legendary downhills.

Not to be outdone, a group of riders in Southern California put on another downhill. What started as a club race has grown into a world-famous event that draws riders from around the globe. Every year the Leaping Lizard Freefall brings together an odd assortment of professional riders, students, business managers and surf bums. The individuals are as diverse as the bicycles they bring with them. Extreme mountain biking is their shared interest. On one weekend each year they race against the clock, trying to be the next champion of a trail the local riders call Telonix.

My stomach turned with excitement as I rolled my bike to the starting line. In just under sixty seconds, I would be speeding down Telonix. The finish line is one and a half kilometres away and three hundred metres below. Between the

LEFT and RIGHT

Competitors in the
Leaping Lizard
Freefall. The
expression you
can see on their
faces is probably
fear.

top and the bottom is a combination of fire roads, rutted dirt tracks, weathered sandstone boulders and muddied hairpin turns. These give the Leaping Lizard Freefall the reputation for being one of the most radical downhill races anywhere.

A lmost fifty speed-merchants wait restlessly with me for their turn to hurl themselves downward. Some of the best bike handlers in the world are among them. Looking about me, the lack of flashy lycra is apparent. These riders judge each other not by

ABOVE

Dave Wonderly, the eventual winner, about to catch some big air off a jump on the second day of racing.

what they wear, but how they perform on the threshold of complete adrenalin overload. Each year the times get faster as the maniacs push their personal limits.

Most have practised the course until every rock, turn and bump is memorized. If they have any time-saving techniques, they keep it to themselves.

'Ten seconds.'

I sucked down deep breaths and focused my eyes on the sandstone under the front tyre. The timer counted

off the last few seconds of sanity.

'5, 4, 3, 2, 1, Go!'

The Leaping Lizard Freefall had begun. In seconds I was pedalling hard and fast over the crest of the hill. The wind roared past my ears and brought tears to my eyes. The cactus and sagebrush lining the course became a blur as I passed the point of no return (well the point of no stopping anyway). Steering the bike through the rocky twists and turns, I feathered the brakes only enough to stay in control. At this speed even a

LEFT

Most competitors practise the course until every twist and turn is memorized.

small mistake would send me flying off the trail and into the cactus. Spectators were gathered near the large boulder section with the hope of watching the riders catching big air off the natural jumps. A rough section near the finish almost tore my hands off the handlebars. I gripped them even tighter than before.

Leg muscles burning and arms numb, I roared past the finish line two minutes and twenty seconds later. Race over, pressure off, I hiked back up the trail to watch those who were following me down. One by one the downhillers flew past on their way to the finish below.

The fastest time of the day was

turned in by Dave Wonderly with a mind-numbing one minute fifty seconds. This new course record beat his previous best by nine seconds, and once again proved that he is truly the champion of Telonix. My two minutes and twenty seconds seemed a little bit slow in comparison, but at least I got down (some people didn't), and I had some serious fun, too.

Racing is not for everyone. It is about pushing yourself to the limits of personal performance. A weird attitude is needed to endure the painful excitement competition delivers. No flash clothing or expensive bike will make you go fast without dedicated training, practice and an unwavering belief in yourself.

Tim Gould, one of the most talented riders in the sport, advises racers to, *'set realistic goals. Start with local events and go from there. It's a long, gradual climb to the top so don't expect to compete at championship levels too soon. Don't get discouraged, and have fun.'*

Those who finish a punishing race

BELOW

Races also go uphill. They're not as fast, but they're even harder work!

LEFT

Sara Ballantine wades towards the end of a tough ride.

have the reward of knowing they did their best. Even if you come in last, you will have learned something about your cycling and will be stronger for having experienced it. You will also have met many new friends.

'Keep things in perspective', says three-time world champion Sara Ballantine. *'See how you're improving race to race rather than comparing yourself with the best in the world. Let your abilities develop naturally.'*

MAINTENANCE

Proper care and maintenance of your bike will increase its life and give hassle-free riding. Mountain bikes get exposed to mud, water and heavy abuse, so they need care and attention if you want them to work properly. Regular maintenance will keep yours functioning like new. It also ensures a safe ride. Speeding downhill is not the time to wonder if you should have replaced those frayed brake cables or checked the noise coming from the headset.

The mountain bike has a lot of pivoting parts, sliding cables and rolling bearings which depend on proper cleaning, lubrication and adjustment to perform well. Although bikes are a simple concept, maintaining one requires special tools and a gentle touch. Bike maintenance skills, like handling skills, develop slowly through patience and practice.

Begin by learning what the components do and how they feel and sound when riding. Familiarize yourself with the functions of the derailleurs, brakes and wheels. Knowing how they work is vital to understanding how to care for your bicycle properly.

The best maintenance is the

Computers are becoming a vital tool to the designers of mountain bikes and their components. Computers can test new designs without the manufacturer building the bike, which saves time and money.

preventive kind. This means you should locate and correct problems before they cause damage. Keeping your bike clean and lubricated is the simplest and most important form of preventive maintenance. Keeping the grease and grime off the moving parts reduces wear, and a clean bike is easier to adjust. A bucket of soapy water and a good brush will take care of wheels, tyres and the crankset. A soapy cloth or sponge should be used on paintwork and an old toothbrush works wonders on small parts.

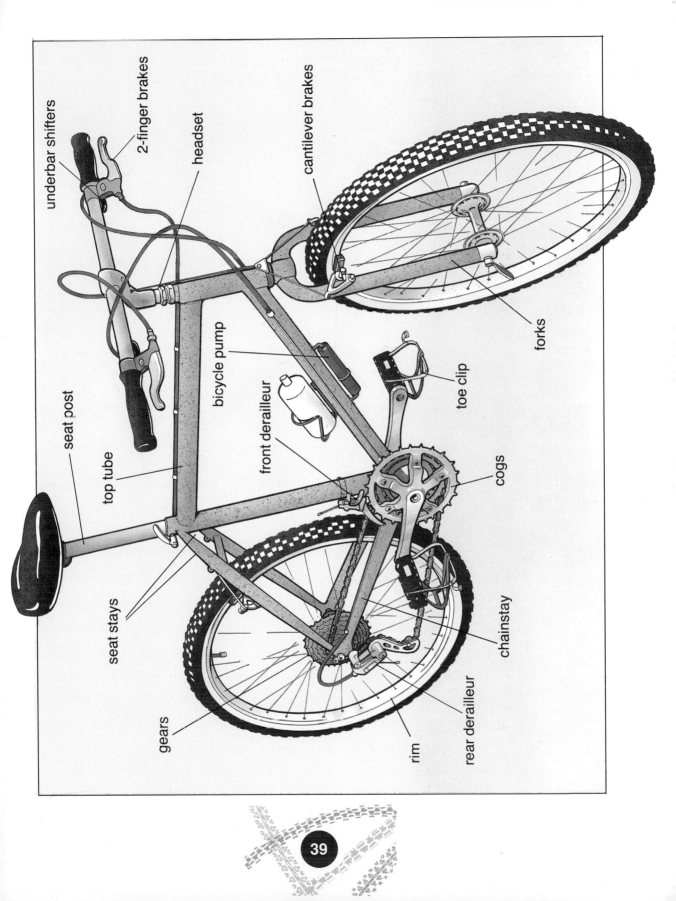

underbar shifters

2-finger brakes

headset

cantilever brakes

forks

seat post

top tube

bicycle pump

front derailleur

toe clip

cogs

seat stays

gears

chainstay

rim

rear derailleur

Ozone-friendly spray solvents will clean the chain and derailleurs.

Be careful when you are rinsing the bike to avoid spraying water around the bottom bracket, headset and hubs. This forces in dirt and water and leads to damage of the bearings. Ask experienced riders how they clean their bike.

While cleaning your bike, check for damage and potential problems. Look out for frayed cables, loose or worn parts and cracks or wrinkles in the paintwork which could indicate a bent or broken frame or forks. Spin the wheels. If the rims rub irregularly against the brake pads, they may be bent, or out of true. If something is loose or out of adjustment, take it to the nearest shop for repair. Ignoring problems can lead to further damage. Every time you ride you trust your life to the quality of maintenance the bike has received. So make a point of keeping it in good shape.

Lubrication is vital. It keeps the moving parts sliding and rolling smoothly. Different components need different lubrication. Chains and derailleurs receive light oils while bearings use thick grease. Many different types of lubrication exist so it is easy to get confused. Ask your bike shop what they recommend for each component.

In addition to keeping the bike clean and lubricated, the parts must be properly adjusted. Each component needs special attention. Parts which are either too loose or tight can cause damage. It takes practice and attention to develop the delicate feel required for proper maintenance. It is a good idea to watch more experienced riders or mechanics working on bikes. You will learn a lot by asking them questions. There are many bike manuals which are a good learning source. One of the best of these manuals is *Richard's New Bicycle Book* by Richard Ballantine.

Tim Davies advises, *'I make sure everything is adjusted and tight before I leave home on a ride. This cuts down problems out on the trail and cuts down on the amount of tools I have to carry.'*

BELOW

Before you go out, check the bike over and make sure everything is working.

LAND ACCESS

A s mountain biking grows so do the problems of land access. Vast areas of public and private land are being closed to mountain biking both in the USA and Europe at an alarming rate. Open, undeveloped land is one of the world's most precious natural resources. Once a piece of land becomes a block of apartments or a golf course, it can never be returned to its original state.

As land development and population grow, outdoor enthusiasts have less and less room. The demand for access to public land is growing as the amount of land decreases.

LEFT

Finding a lonely spot like this is getting harder and harder, as more people want to use the land.

The future holds little relief for this pressure on the land. People will continue to leave their busy lives and cities behind to search for peace and serenity in the country lands and on the mountain trails.

The popularity of mountain biking has made it easier for more people to get out to enjoy the great outdoors. They are using many areas traditionally used by both hikers and horse riders. The established users view the increasing number of mountain bikers as unwanted invaders of their favourite spots. In many cases, this conflict has led to land closures for mountain bikes. Many of these problems were caused by a few unthinking individuals who give all mountain bikers a bad name. Every rider has to act in such a way that further closures are prevented.

Y ou will be sharing the trails with many different users, so be on the look-out. When you meet a hiker or horse rider, give them the right of way. Do not skid or yell to get their attention. They are there for the

The strong frame and wheels, good brakes and multiple gears of the mountain bike make it a good bike for touring. From a long day trip to a trans-continental ride, cyclists are continually exploring the less-travelled places of our world. Special packs called panniers can be carried. They might contain a tent, a sleeping bag, food and clothes.

RIGHT

Be careful of other countryside users such as horse riders. They have a right to be there too.

peace and quiet. When approaching others, be prepared to slow and stop if necessary to let them pass. Be especially careful when dealing with horses. Give them plenty of room and make no sudden movements. Some people will get out of your way, but do not expect it. Be sure to thank them if they do. Above all, be friendly. Just because a hiker interrupted your favourite descent does not give you the right to be angry. They are allowed to be there too. Other people are not the enemy, they are your partners in using and caring for the land.

RIGHT and BELOW

Because of damage to the land, large areas in Europe and the USA are being closed to riders.

During your offroad travel, you will encounter people who will not like mountain biking and will tell you so. It is not worth arguing with these people. It is best just to say, 'I'm sorry you feel that way.' And keep riding.

Respect closed areas. If you are in doubt, get permission. Sneaking on to illegal trails will only damage mountain biking's already tarnished image. There will be times when your favourite trail is too crowded to enjoy. Look for another time or place to ride. A Sunday afternoon on the local bridleway may not be the best time for a hard training ride. If you need the speed, investigate the local race scene, or start one up if it does not exist already.

As well as dealing with other users, you must be aware of how the mountain bike can affect the environment. While tearing a new path cross-country is hard to resist, this sort of riding severely damages vegetation, which leads to erosion. It takes years for nature to heal just a moment of thoughtlessness. Stay on the established trails and leave those untracked meadows and steep hill sides for viewing not riding.

Try not to lock up your wheels just to skid for fun. Tyre tracks can create channels for water and cause erosion. Test your handling skills by controlling your speed without locking up. Switchback turns are designed to channel water away from the trail and cutting the corners can lead to irreparable damage. While burying your bike up to the axles on a muddy trail may be fun, think about the damage you are causing the trail.

Pack out what you have packed in. Leaving no trace of your presence should be your goal. By developing an attitude and cycling skills which reduce the bicycle's impact on the environment, you will be keeping mountain biking areas open.

BELOW

Would you want to ride through wasteland like this? If not, it is in your interest to co-operate with other land users and try to prevent erosion or 'development'.

GLOSSARY

Allen key, also hex key   A six-sided tool used in many adjustments on a mountain bike. The most common sizes are 4, 5 and 6 mm.

Bottom bracket   The assembly that connects the crankset to the frame.

Bunny hop   Lifting both wheels off the ground at the same time.

Cadence   The speed at which the pedals spin.

Cantilever brakes   The most common type of brakes on mountain bikes. Mounted on the forks and seat stays, they work as levers and are more powerful and easier to adjust than other types.

Chain breaker   A tool used to press in and out the pins which hold the links of the chain together.

Coaster brakes   An early type of brake that was applied by pedalling backwards.

Cogs   The part of the driving mechanism at the back of the bike that has teeth, on which the chain catches.

Crankset   The arms to which the pedals and bottom bracket are connected.

Dehydration   A condition that occurs when your body loses too much water.

Dual slalom   A race where riders compete head-to-head (next to one another), going through gates as in a ski race.

Feathering   A method of braking where the front and rear levers are gently squeezed on and off to control speed and prevent wheel skid.

Freewheel   The assembly that supports the gears, or cogs, on the rear wheel. It lets the wheel turn without the pedals going round.

Friction shifter   A type of shifter that moves smoothly without the click of indexed shifting.

Gears   *See cogs.*

Headset   The set of bearings located at either end of the head tube. Used to connect the forks to the frame.

Indexed shifter   A type of gear shifter where a click of the shift lever corresponds with a change of gear.

Quick release   A device using a lever and skewer which is used instead of a nut and bolt on wheel axles and seat posts for easy removal or adjustment.

Seat pack   A small bag which fits under the saddle, used to carry tools, a spare tube and a patch kit.

Switchback turn   A very tight turn that leads a road going back in almost the direction it came from, in a zigzag.

Toe clip   A device attached to the pedal that holds the foot in the proper position and gives greater power to the pedal spin.

True   In line. Used to describe a wheel without bumps or bends in the rim.

Wheelie   Riding on the rear wheel or pulling the front wheel off the ground.

Videos

UK
Stadium Videos Europe Ltd.
10 Tonbridge Close
Macclesfield, Cheshire
SK10 3BH
Tel: 0625-32775

USA
Range of Light Productions
PO Box 2906
Mammoth Lakes, CA
93546
Tel: 619-935-4648

Mountain Biking Organizations

Australia
Australian Mountain Bike Association
PO Box N25
Grosvenor Place
Sydney NSW 2000

Canada
Canadian Cycling Association
1600 James Naismith Drive
Gloucester
Ontario K1B 5N4

New Zealand
New Zealand Mountain Bike Association
PO Box 371
Taupo

UK
UK Mountain Bike Federation
36 Rockingham Road
Kettering
Northants NN16 8HG

Vixens is a mountain biking network that puts women and girls in touch at a local level.
Vixens
1 Whitegates Road
Cheadle
Cheshire SK8 1EA

USA
National Off-road Bicycle Association
1750 E Boulder
Colorado Springs
CO 80909

Index